**Directions**: Review each image, word and alphabet daily.

Day 1

# Aa

Apple

A

a

A

a

**Directions**: Review each image, word and alphabet daily.

Day 1

# Aa

Apple

A

a

A

a

**Directions**: Review each image, word and alphabet daily.

Day 2

# Bb

Baseball

B

b

B

b

**Directions**: Review each image, word and alphabet daily.

Day 2

# Bb

Baseball

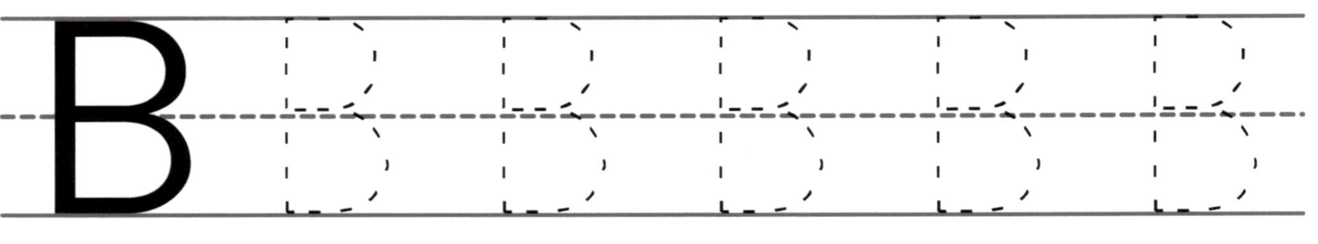

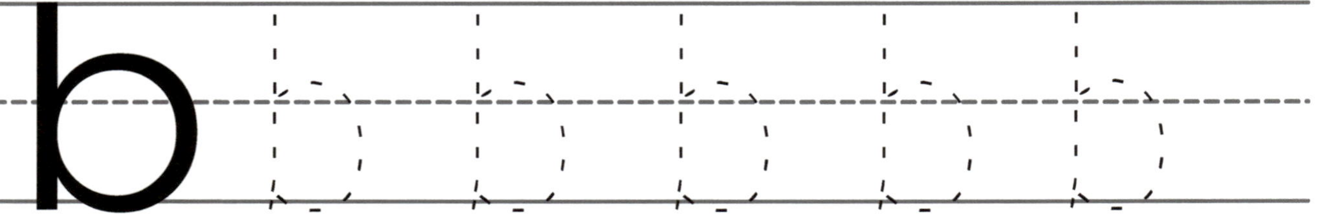

B

b

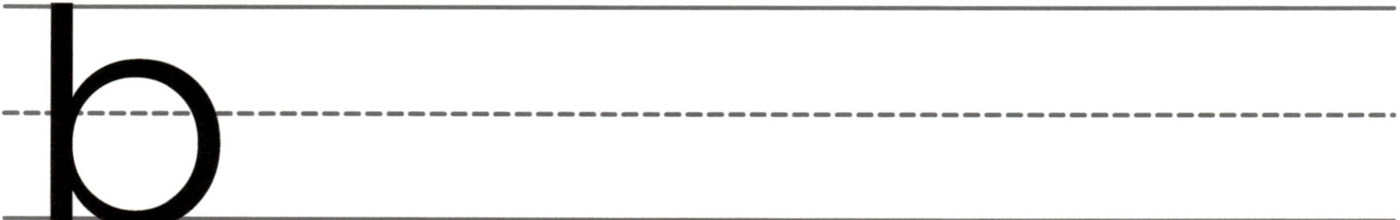

**Directions**: Review each image, word and alphabet daily.

Day 3

# Cc

Couch

C

C

C

c

**Directions**: Review each image, word and alphabet daily.

Day 3

# Cc

Couch

C

c

C

c

**Directions**: Review each image, word and alphabet daily.

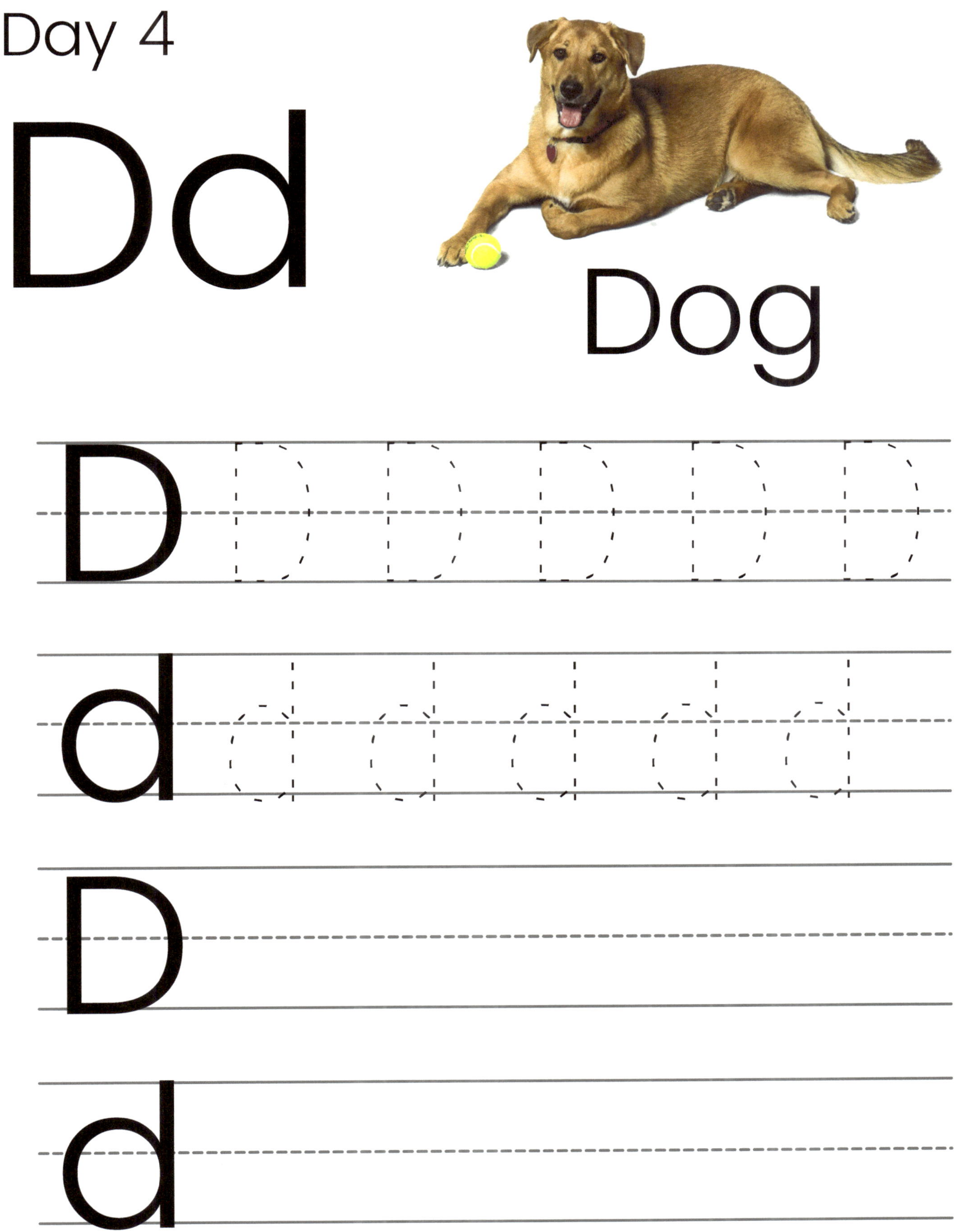

**Directions**: Review each image, word and alphabet daily.

Day 4

# Dd

Dog

D

d

D

d

**Directions**: Review each image, word and alphabet daily.

Day 5

# Ee

Elephant

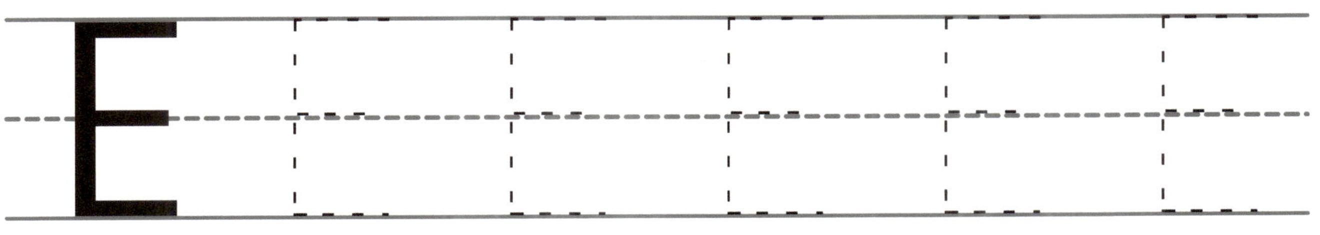

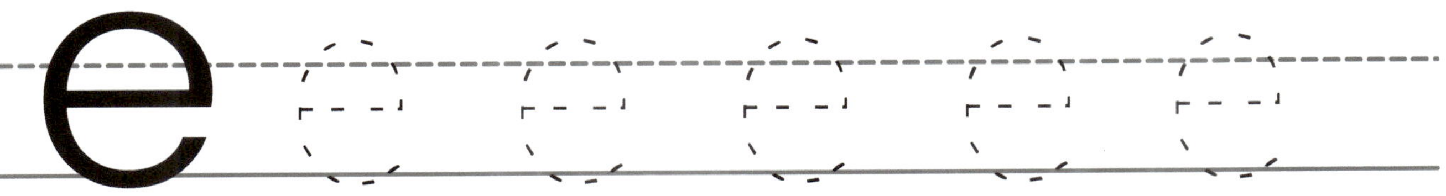

E

**Directions**: Review each image, word and alphabet daily.

Day 5

# Ee

Elephant

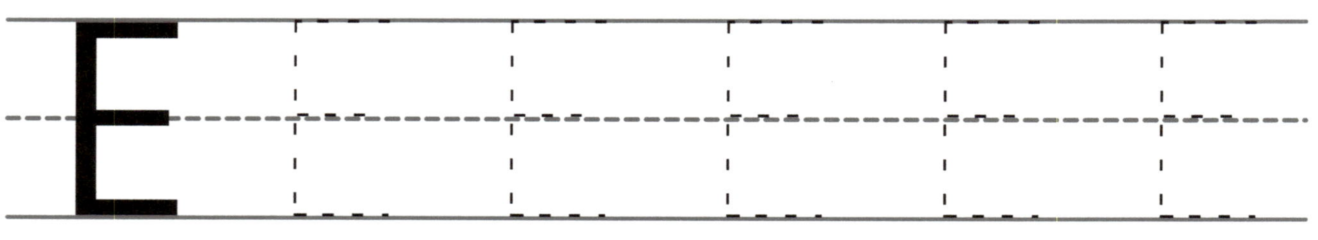

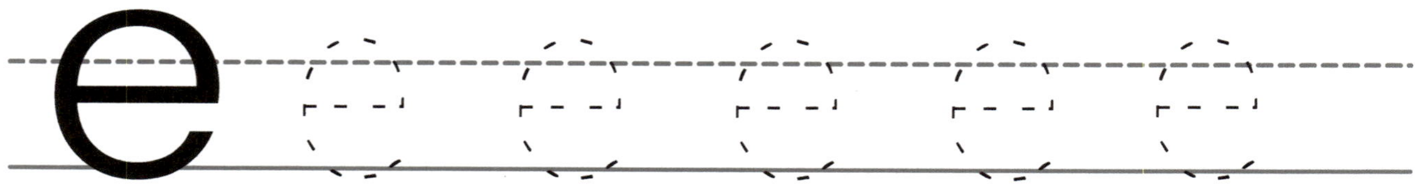

E

**Directions**: Review each image, word and alphabet daily.

Day 6

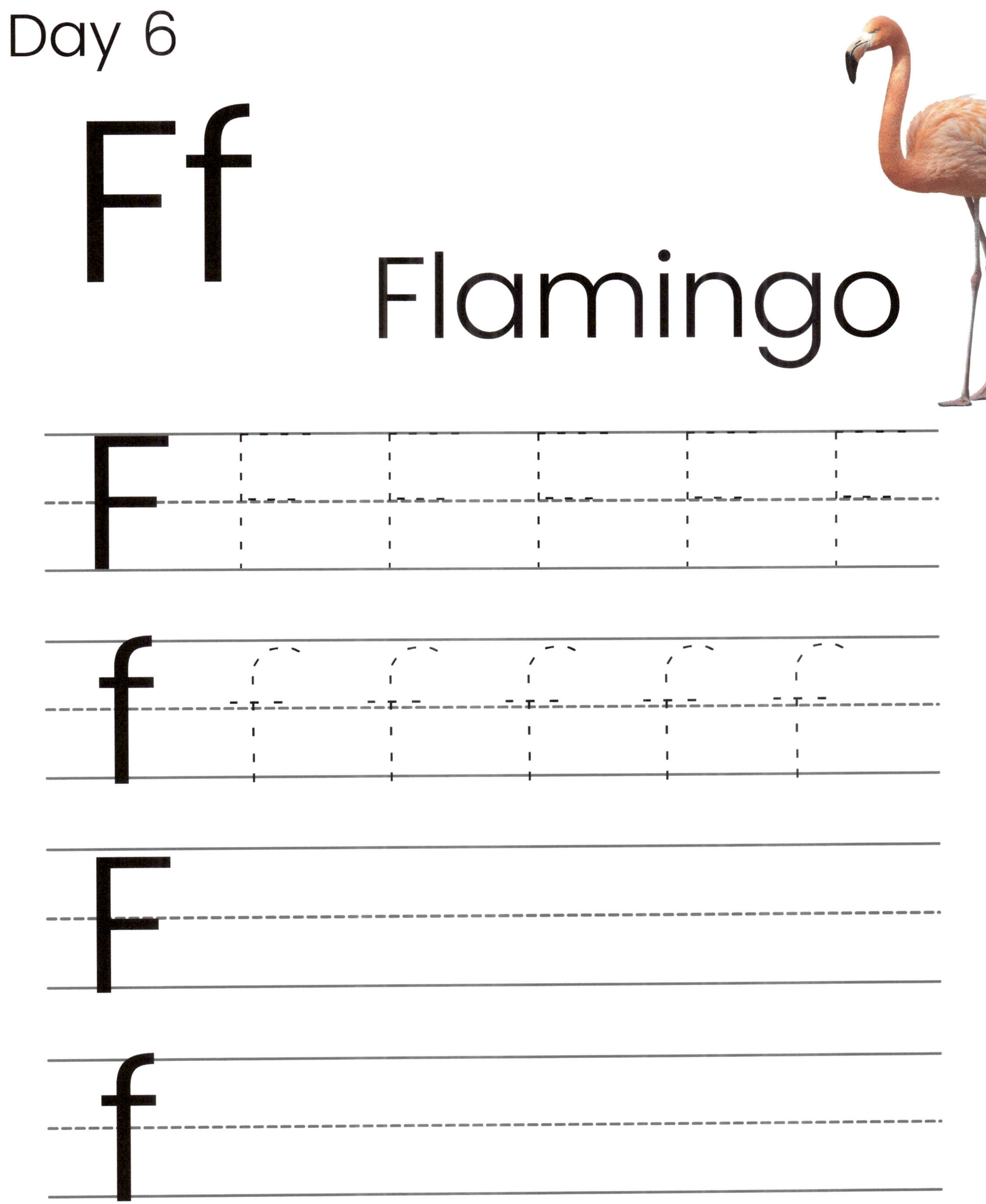

**Directions**: Review each image, word and alphabet daily.

Day 6

**Directions**: Review each image, word and alphabet daily.

Day 7

# Gg

Gorilla

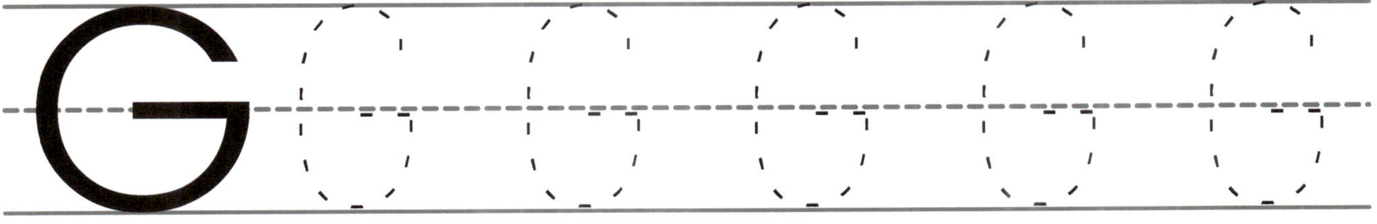

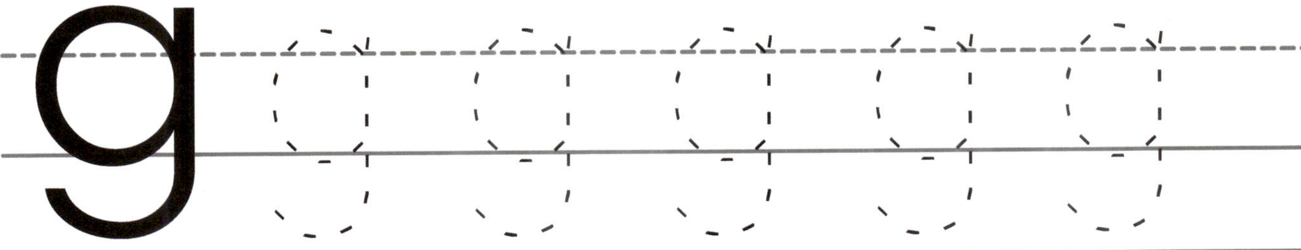

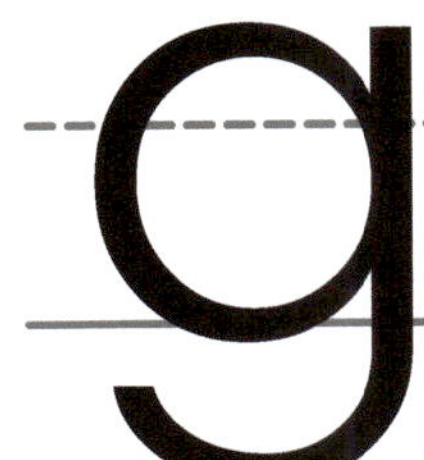

**Directions**: Review each image, word and alphabet daily.

Day 7

# Gg

## Gorilla

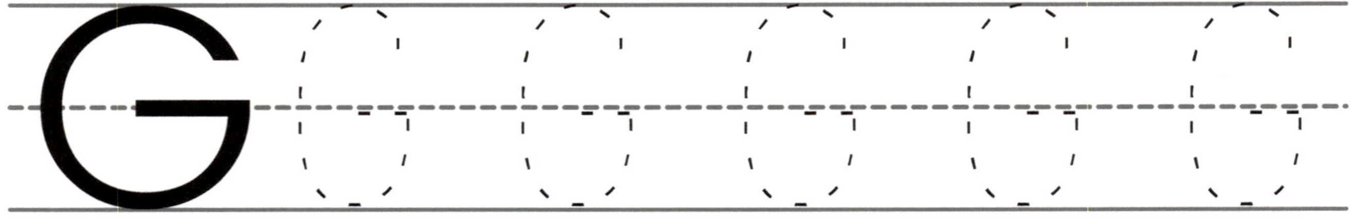

g

G

g

**Directions**: Review each image, word and alphabet daily.

Day 8

# Hh

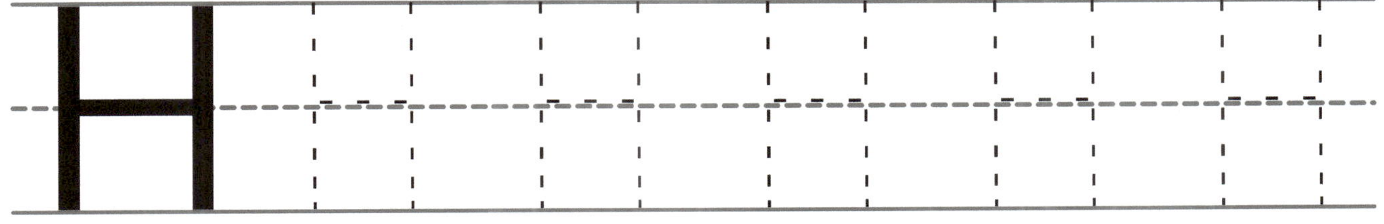


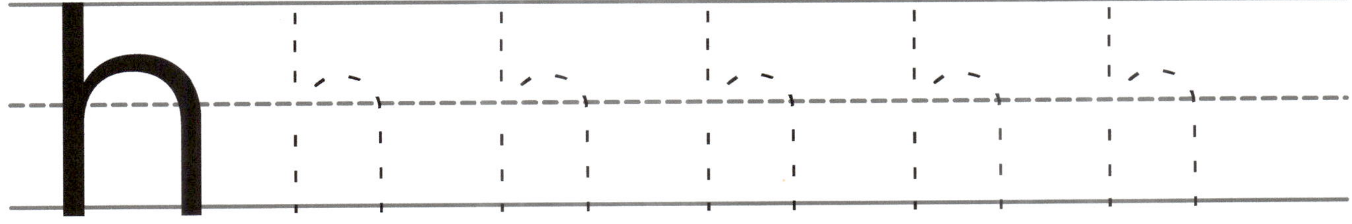

**Directions**: Review each image, word and alphabet daily.

Day 8

Horse

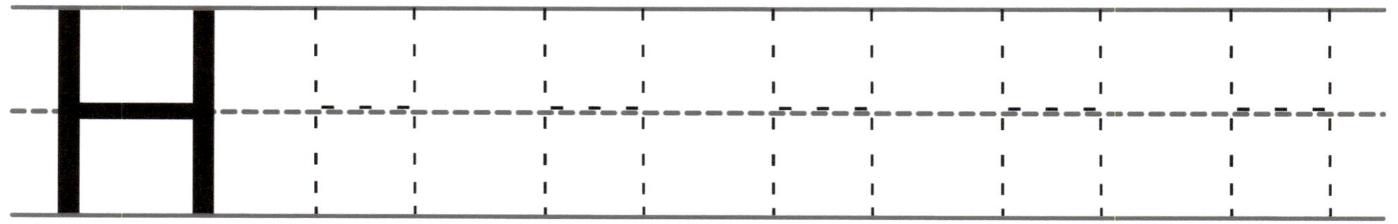

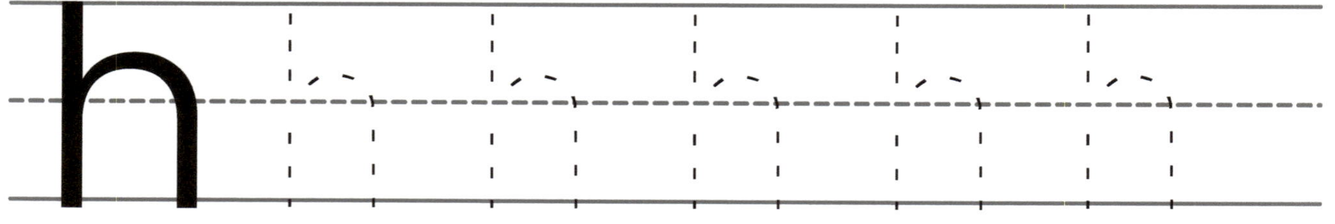

**Directions**: Review each image, word and alphabet daily.

Day 9

# Ii

Igloo

I

i

I

i

**Directions**: Review each image, word and alphabet daily.

Day 9

# Ii

Igloo

I

i

I

i

**Directions**: Review each image, word and alphabet daily.

Day 10

**Directions**: Review each image, word and alphabet daily.

**Directions**: Review each image, word and alphabet daily.

Day 11

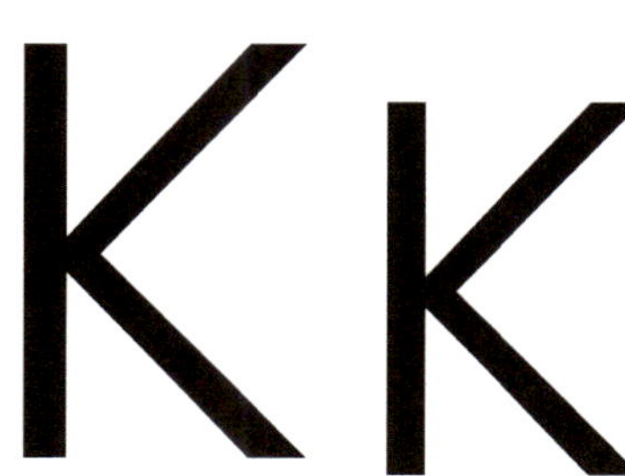

Kitten

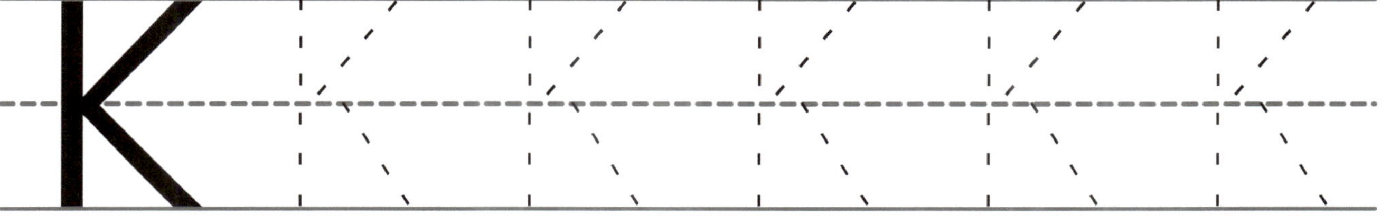

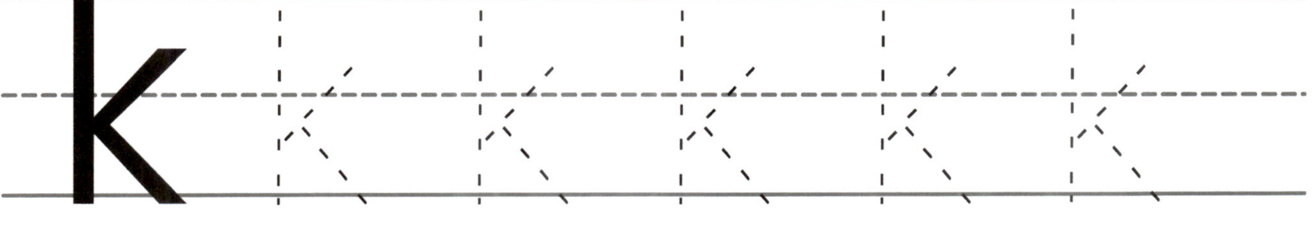

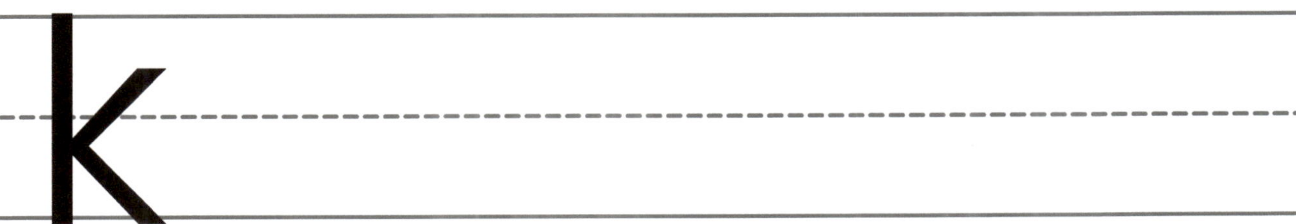

**Directions**: Review each image, word and alphabet daily.

Day 11

# K k

Kitten

K

k

K

k

**Directions**: Review each image, word and alphabet daily.

Day 12

# Ll

Leaf

L

l

L

l

**Directions**: Review each image, word and alphabet daily.

**Directions**: Review each image, word and alphabet daily.

Day 13

Money

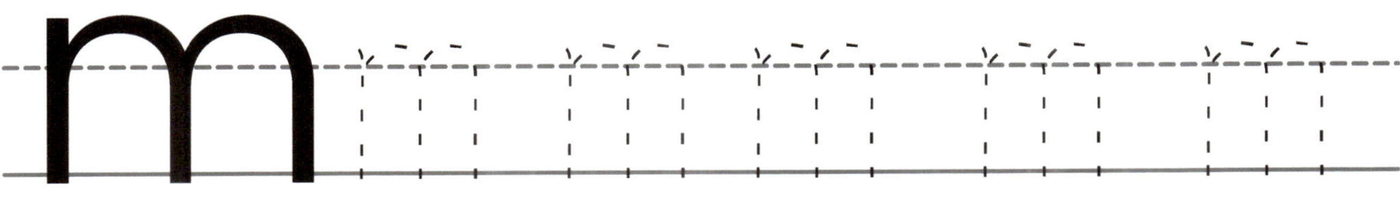

**Directions**: Review each image, word and alphabet daily.

# Day 13

# Mm

## Money

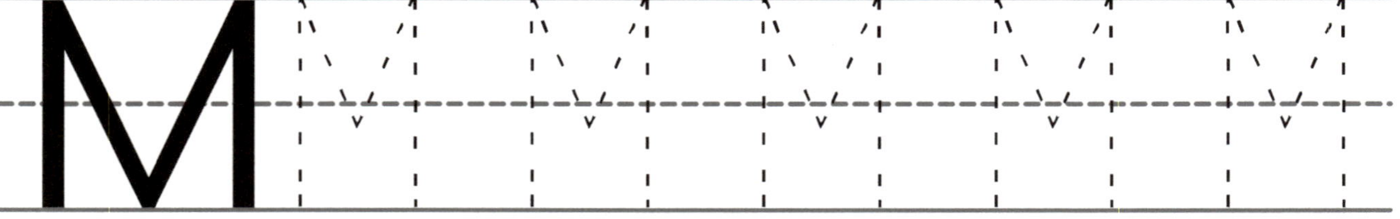

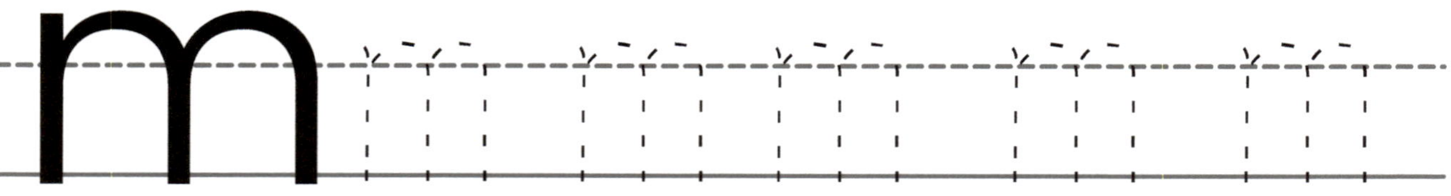

**Directions**: Review each image, word and alphabet daily.

Day 14

# Nn

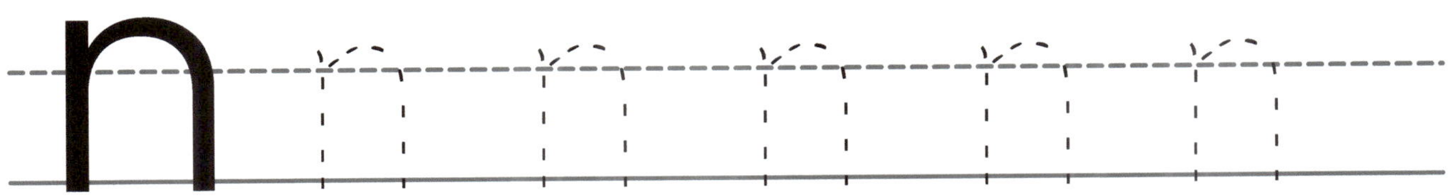


N

n

**Directions**: Review each image, word and alphabet daily.

Day 14

# Nn

Nest

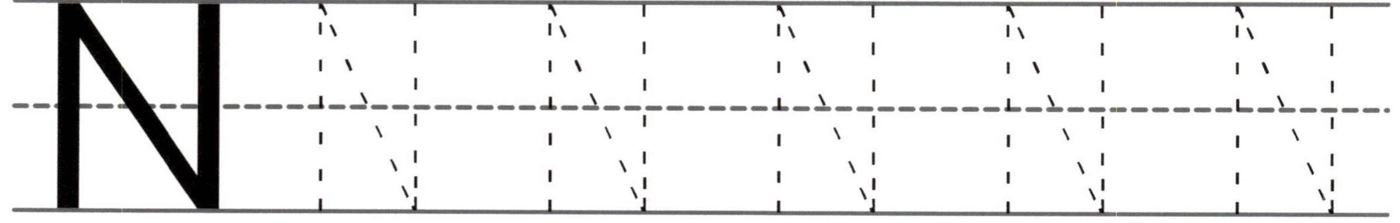

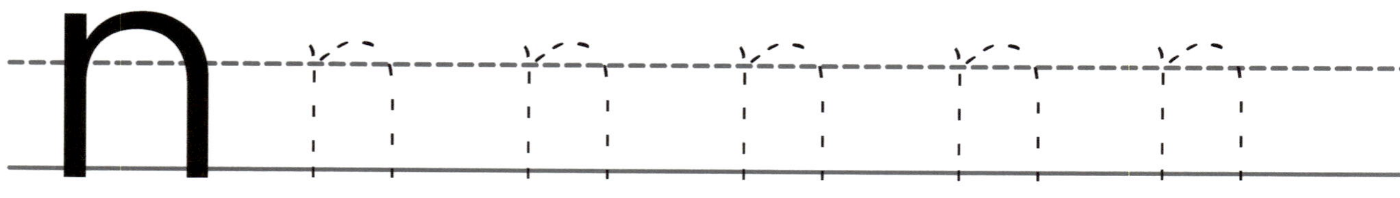

**Directions**: Review each image, word and alphabet daily.

Day 15

# Oo

Owl

**Directions**: Review each image, word and alphabet daily.

Day 15

# Oo

Owl

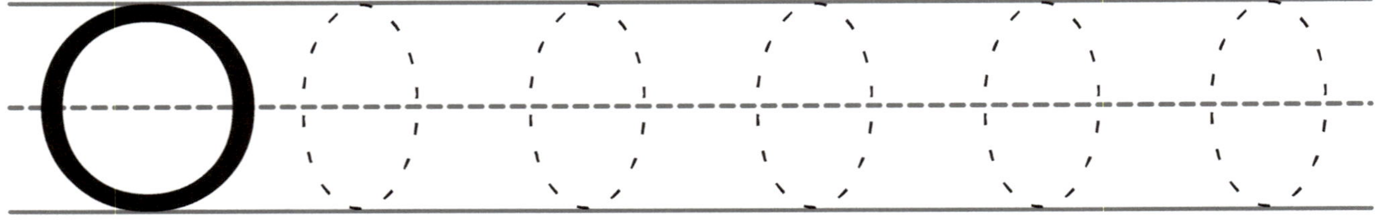

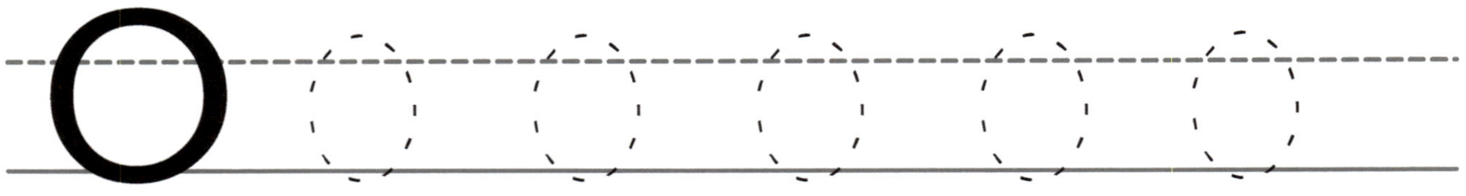

**Directions**: Review each image, word and alphabet daily.

Day 16

# Pp

Penguin

P

p

P

p

**Directions**: Review each image, word and alphabet daily.

Day 16

# Pp

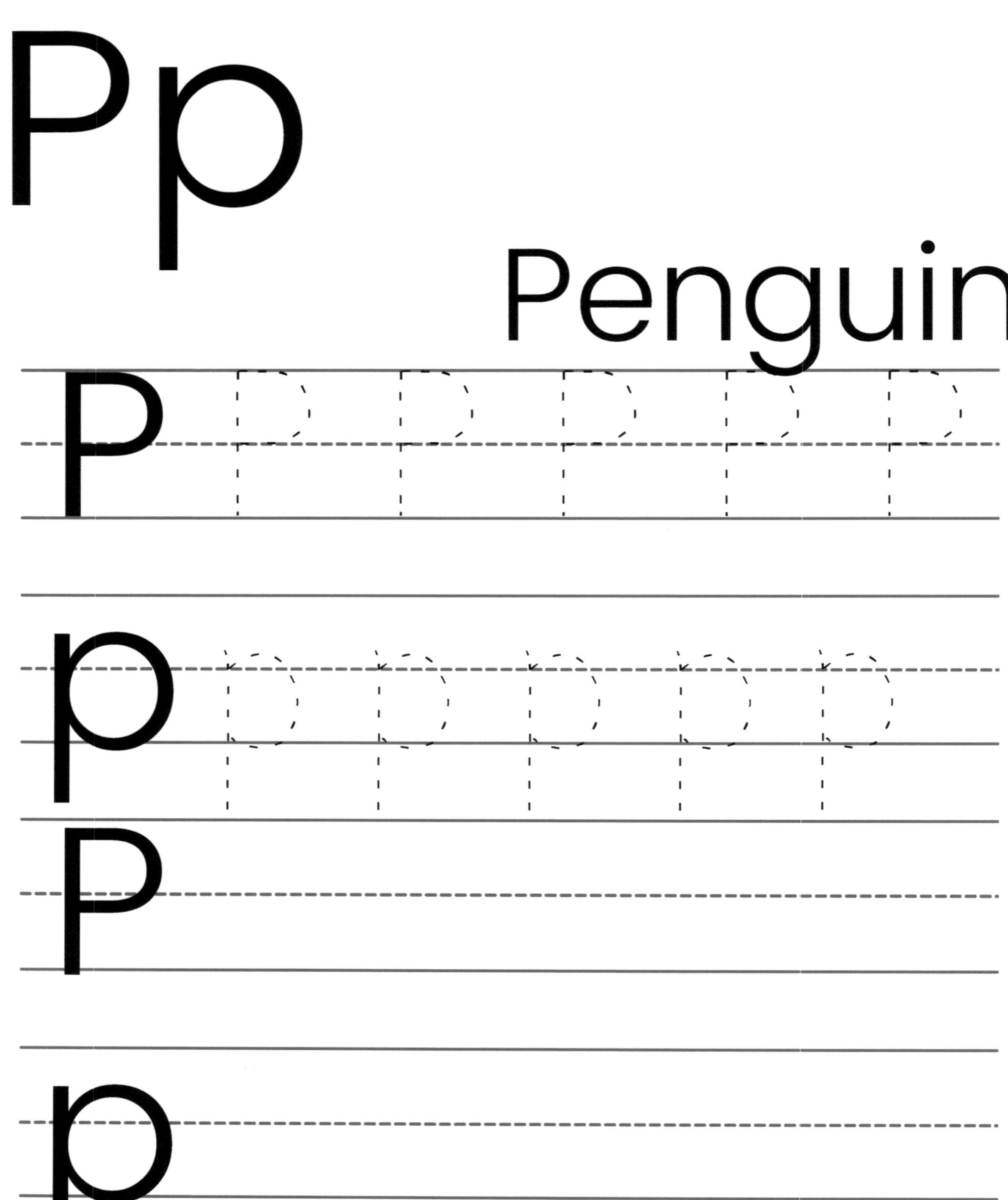

**Directions**: Review each image, word and alphabet daily.

Day 17

# Qq

Queen

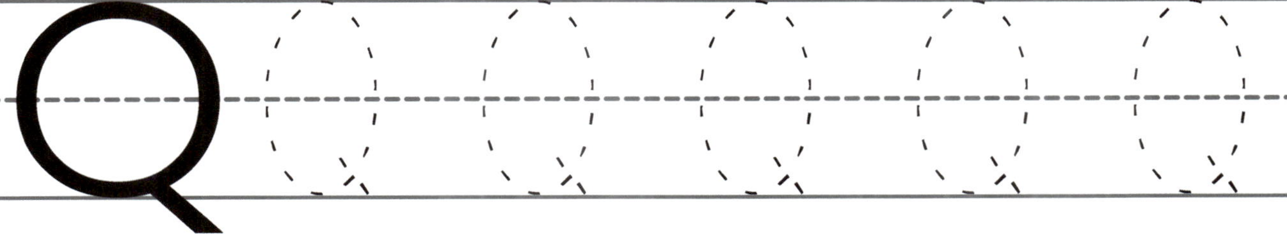

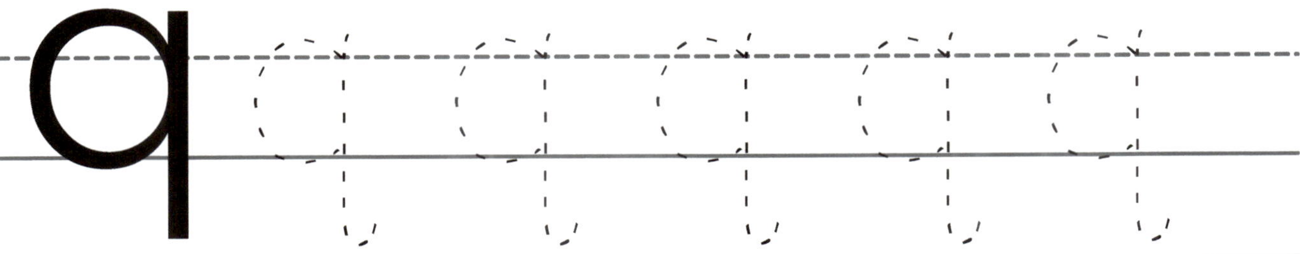

**Directions**: Review each image, word and alphabet daily.

Day 17

# Qq

Queen

Q

q

Q

q

**Directions**: Review each image, word and alphabet daily.

Day 18

# Rr

Rainbow

R

r

R

r

**Directions**: Review each image, word and alphabet daily.

Day 18

# Rr

Rainbow

R

r

R

r

**Directions**: Review each image, word and alphabet daily.

Day 19

# Ss

Sunflower

S

s

S

s

**Directions**: Review each image, word and alphabet daily.

Day 19

# Ss

Sunflower

S

s

S

s

**Directions**: Review each image, word and alphabet daily.

Day 20

# Tt

Table

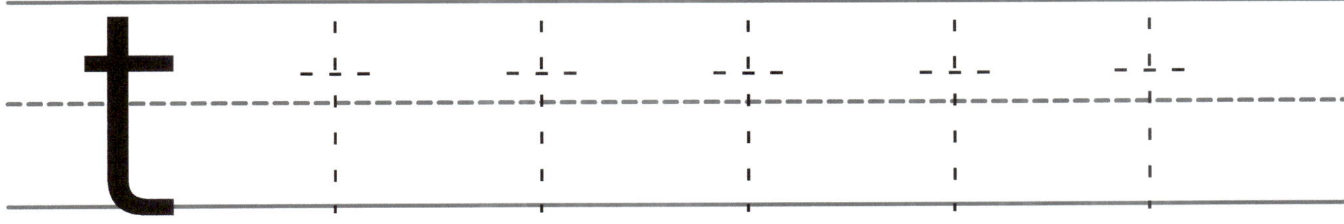

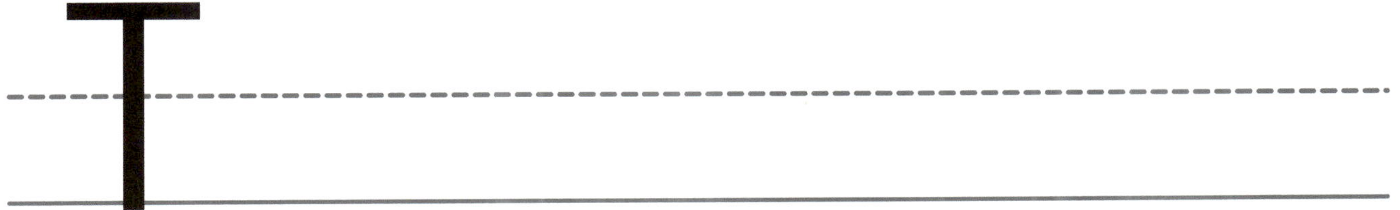

t

**Directions**: Review each image, word and alphabet daily.

Day 20

# Tt

Table

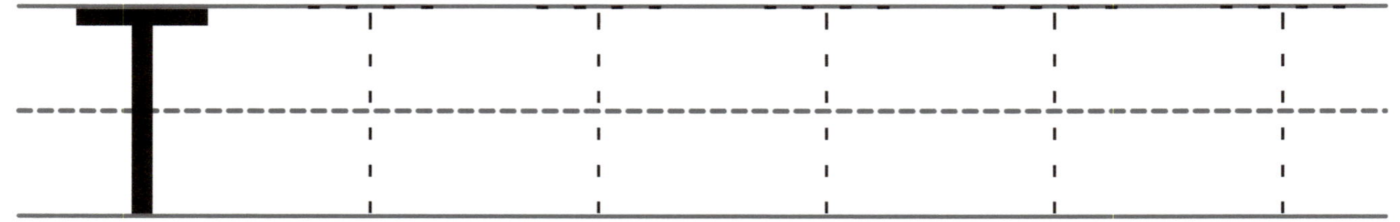


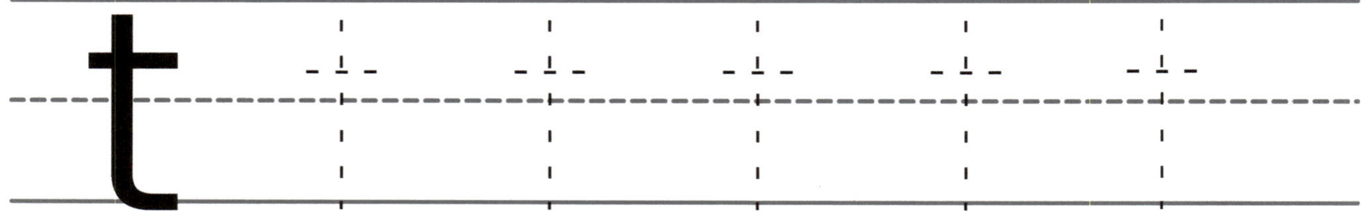

**Directions**: Review each image, word and alphabet daily.

Day 21

# Uu

Umbrella

U

u

U

u

**Directions**: Review each image, word and alphabet daily.

Day 21

# Uu

Umbrella

U

u

U

u

**Directions**: Review each image, word and alphabet daily.

Day 22

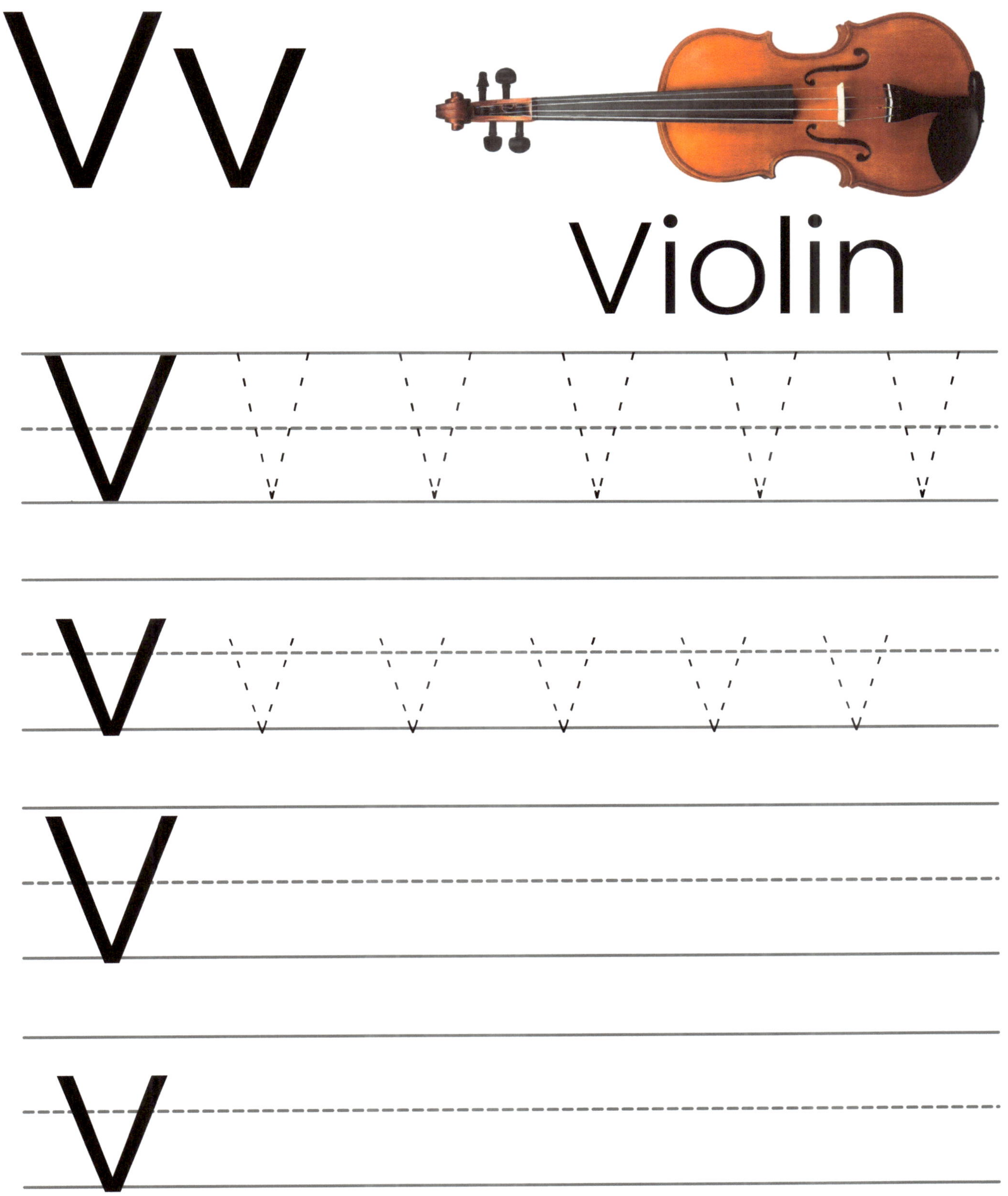

**Directions**: Review each image, word and alphabet daily.

Day 22

**Directions**: Review each image, word and alphabet daily.

Day 23

# Ww

Watermelon

W

w

W

w

**Directions**: Review each image, word and alphabet daily.

Day 23

# Ww

Watermelon

W

w

W

w

**Directions**: Review each image, word and alphabet daily.

Day 24

# Xx

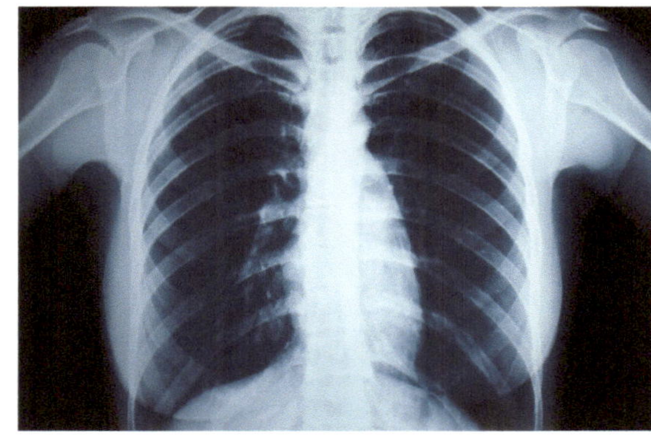

x-ray

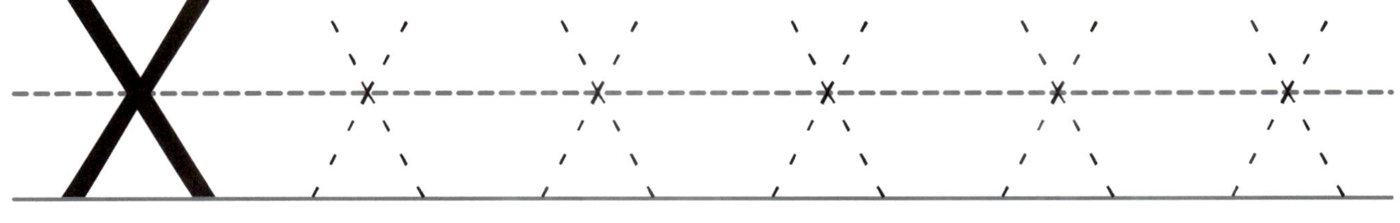

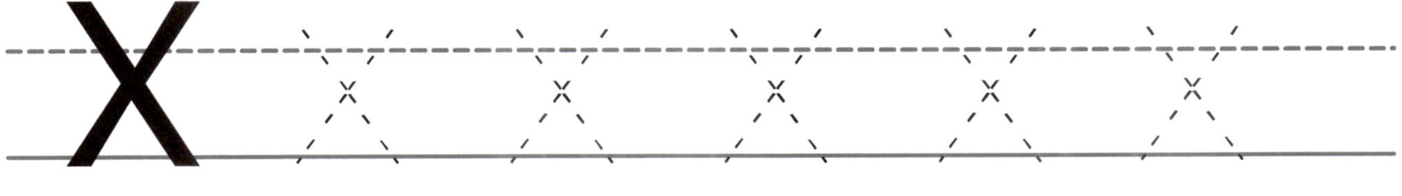

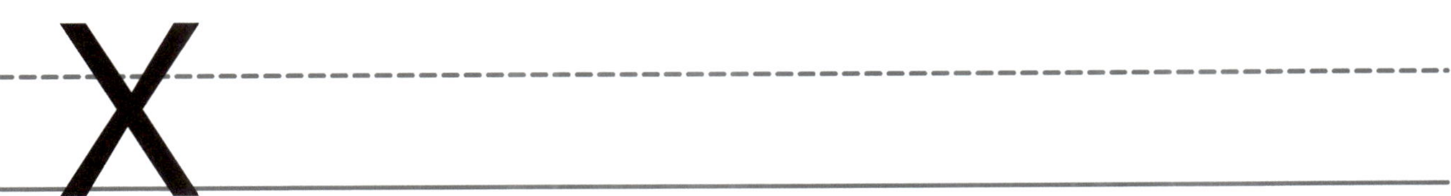

**Directions**: Review each image, word and alphabet daily.

Day 24

# Xx

x-ray

X x x x x x

x x x x x x

X

x

**Directions**: Review each image, word and alphabet daily.

Day 25

# Yy

Yarn

Y

y

Y

y

**Directions**: Review each image, word and alphabet daily.

Day 25

# Yy

Yarn

Y

y

Y

y

**Directions**: Review each image, word and alphabet daily.

Day 26

# Zz

Zebra

Z

z

Z

z

**Directions**: Review each image, word and alphabet daily.

# Day 26

# Zz

## Zebra

Z

z

Z

z

**Directions**: Now it's time for some additional practice. Trace the word apple. Do your best, you got this.

Day 27

# Apple

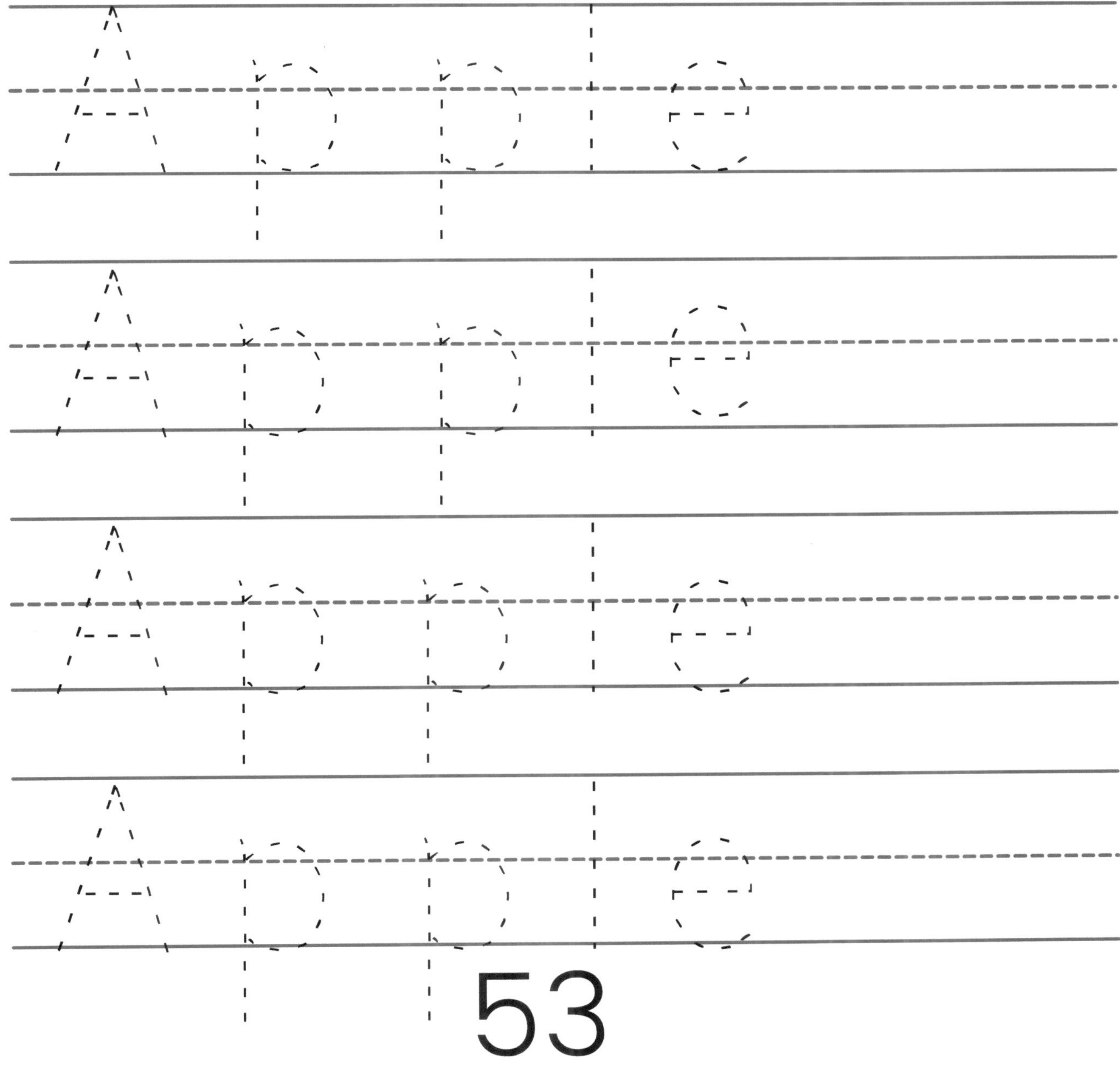

**Directions**: Now it's time for some additional practice. Trace the word apple. Do your best, you got this.

Day 27

# Apple

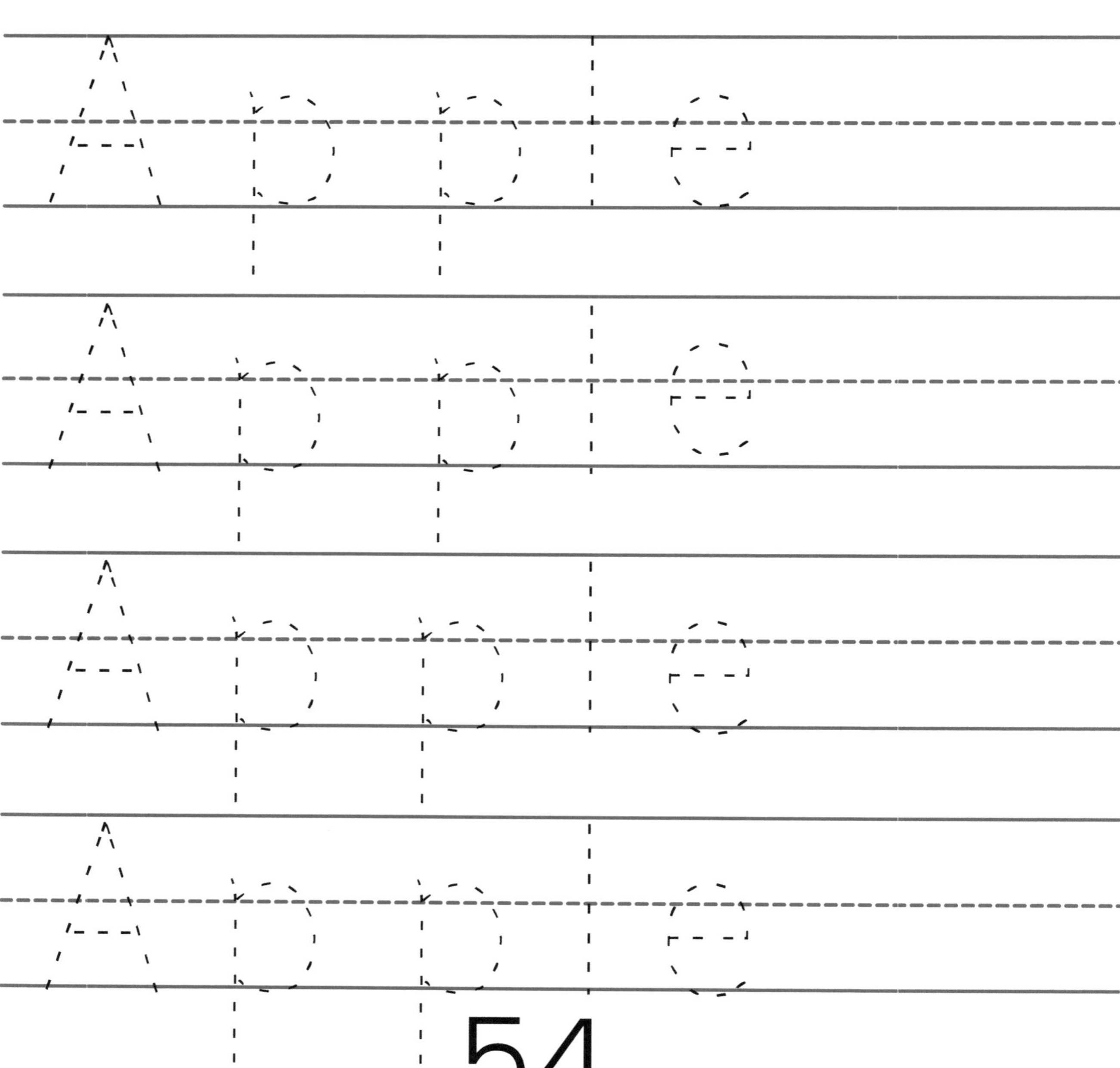

**Directions**: Now it's time for some additional practice. Trace the word table. Do your best, you got this.

Day 28

# Table

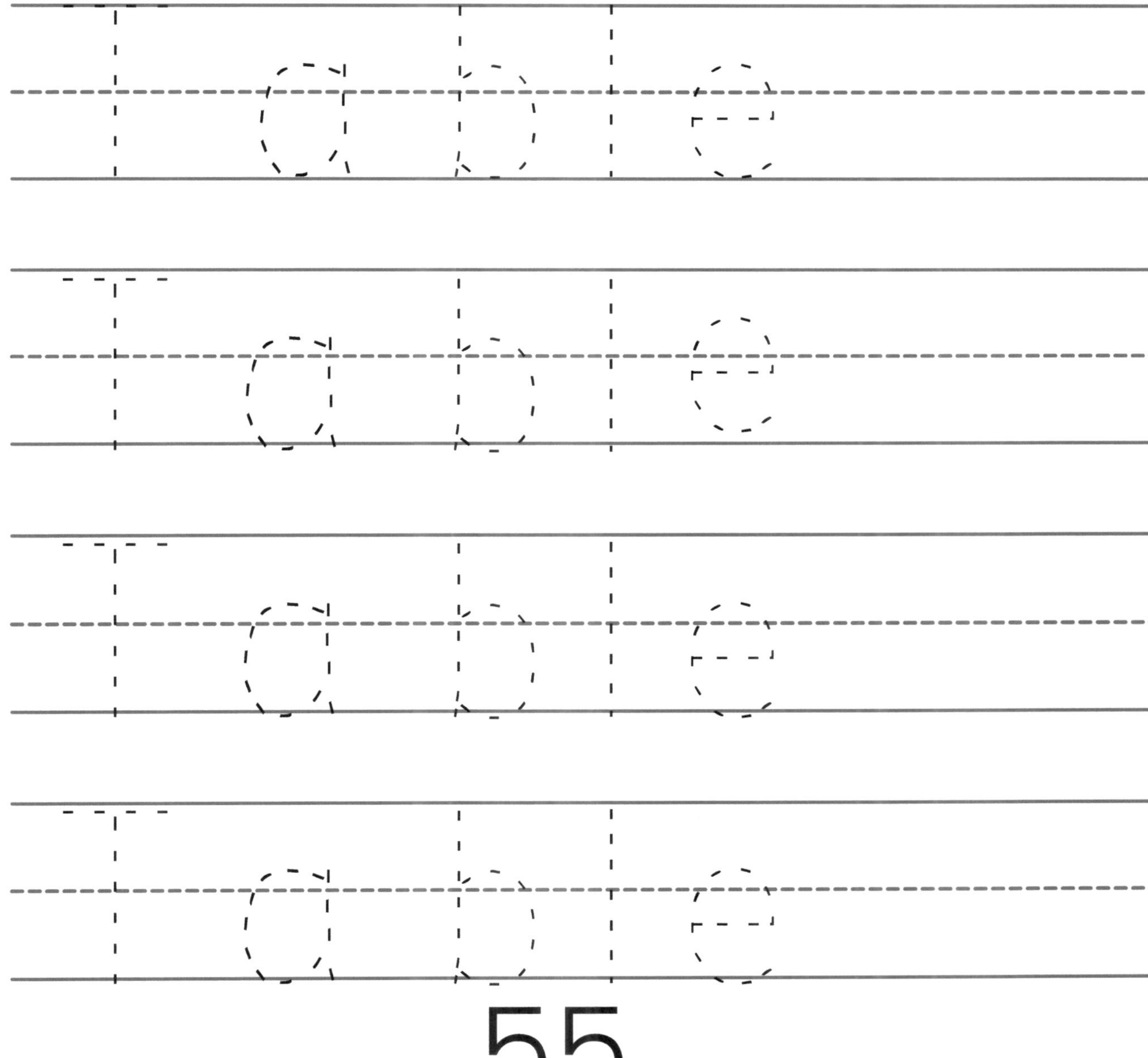

**Directions**: Now it's time for some additional practice. Trace the word table. Do your best, you got this.

Day 28

# Table

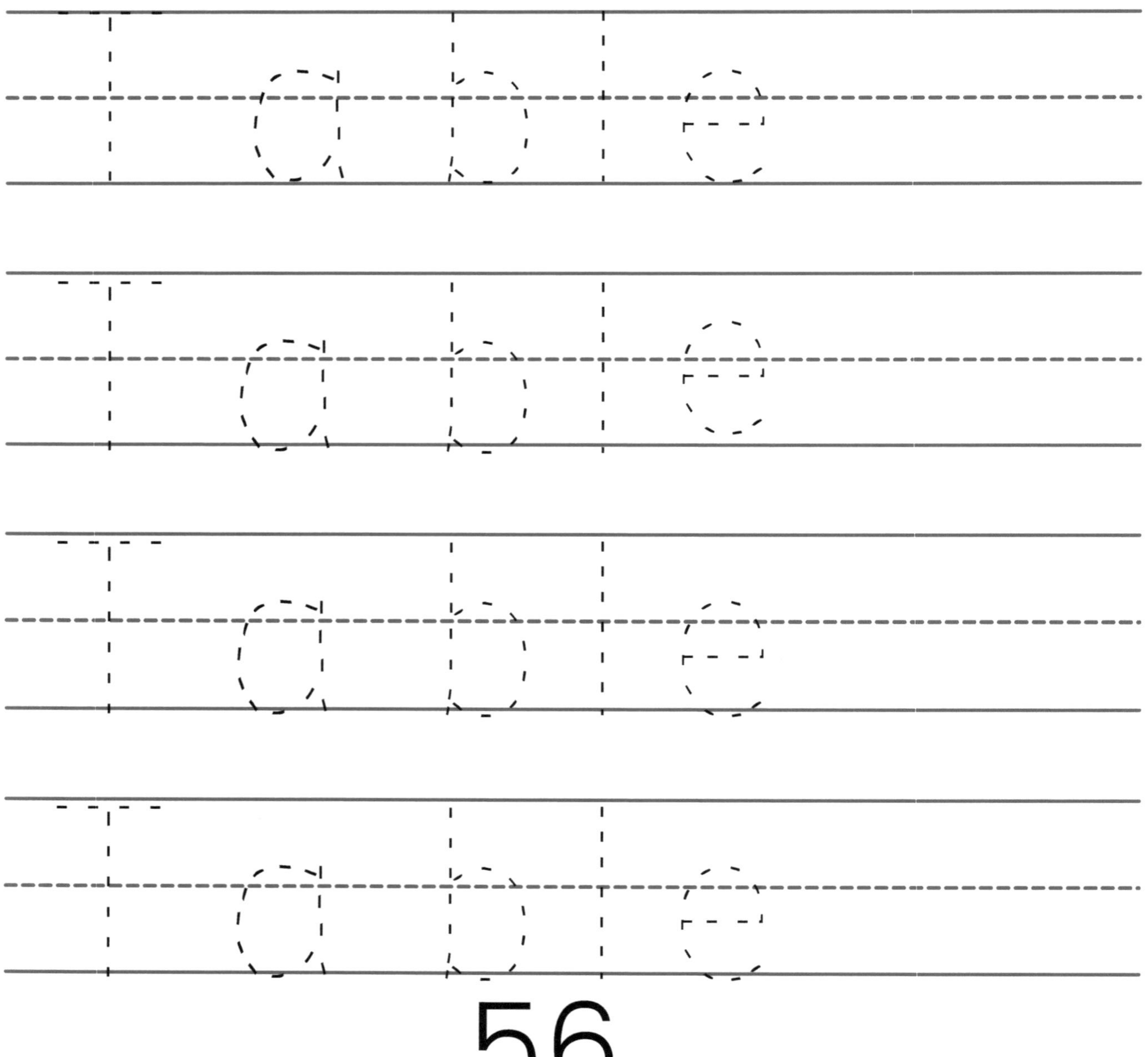

**Directions**: Now it's time for some additional practice. Use the lines below to write your name.

# Day 29

**Directions**: Now it's time for some additional practice. Use the lines below to write your name.

# Day 29

**Directions**: Now it's time for some additional practice. Use the lines below to write your name.

# Day 30

**Directions**: Now it's time for some additional practice. Use the lines below to write your name.

# Day 30

www.ingramcontent.com/pod-product-compliance
Ingram Content Group UK Ltd.
Pitfield, Milton Keynes, MK11 3LW, UK
UKHW060121300726
14090UKWH00002B/291

* 9 7 9 8 7 4 0 0 1 2 1 1 7 *